Mashrak-el-Azkar

Also from Westphalia Press
westphaliapress.org

Mashrak-el-Azkar

Descriptive of the Bahai Temple and Illustrative of an Exhibition of Preliminary Designs for the First Mashrak-el-Azkar to be Built in America

by Charles Mason Remey

WESTPHALIA PRESS
An imprint of Policy Studies Organization

Mashrak-el-Azkar: Descriptive of the Bahai Temple and Illustrative of an Exhibition of Preliminary Designs for the First Mashrak-el-Azkar to be Built in America

Westphalia Press
An imprint of Policy Studies Organization
1527 New Hampshire Ave., NW
Washington, D.C. 20036
info@ipsonet.org

ISBN-13: 978-1-63391-708-8
ISBN-10: 1-63391-708-8

Cover design by Jeffrey Barnes:
jbarnesbook.design

Daniel Gutierrez-Sandoval, Executive Director
PSO and Westphalia Press

Updated material and comments on this edition
can be found at the Westphalia Press website:
www.westphaliapress.org

MASHRAK-EL-AZKAR

Descriptive of the Bahai Temple
———————— and ————————
Illustrative of an exhibition of
preliminary designs for the first
Mashrak-El-Azkar to be built in
America, showing nine varying
treatments in different styles of
architecture

BY

CHARLES MASON REMEY

1917

IN the Persian and Arabic languages each letter has a numerical value and each name or word has as its numerical value the sum of the values of its component letters. B–2—A–1—H–5—A–1. Thus 9 is the numerical value of the name "Baha". This number, which is the greatest of simple numbers, is used by the Bahais as a symbol of name.

Copies of this book may be obtained from the

BAHAI PUBLISHING SOCIETY

P. O. BOX 283, CHICAGO, ILL.

Price   -   - $1.00

Postage extra.

Weight of book 2 pounds.

PRINTED BY
J. D. MILANS & SONS
WASHINGTON, D. C

"MASHRAK-EL-AZKAR."

Literally translated from the Persian "The Dawning Point of the Mentionings (or commemorations) of God."

It is the Bahai Temple with its various auxiliary institutions educational and philanthropic

To ABDUL BAHA
THE SERVANT OF THE SERVANTS OF GOD"
THESE DESIGNS ARE HUMBLY OFFERED

NOTE

———

Those portions of the text of this book which pertain to the Bahai Movement are quoted from various authentic and approved Bahai publications.

CONTENTS

CONTENTS

PREFACE

PREFACE

This book is descriptive of the Mashrak-El-Azkar and is illustrative of an exhibition of nine preliminary designs for the first Mashrak-El-Azkar to be built in America.

These drawings, which represent study and work done at intervals during the past seven or eight years, are offered to Abdul Baha, and intrusted to the keeping of the "Bahai Temple Unity," the organization which has for its object the erection of the first Mashrak-El-Azkar in America, in the hope that some of the elements of these architectural compositions may be of service when the time arrives for formulating and composing the building design for the Mashrak-El-Azkar.

C. M. R.

July, 1917.
Washington, D. C.

I.

INTRODUCTION.

HISTORICAL SKETCH OF THE BAHAI MOVEMENT.

Quoted from "Constructive Principles of the Bahai Teachings."

Chapter III.

THE BAHAI MOVEMENT.

Religion, which is inherent in man, dates in general essence before the dawn of written history, each religious movement in its purity of truth being a phase of the one great Universal divine religion.

The particular present latter-day phase of religion that we are here considering, the Bahai Movement, began over seventy years ago, when its first teacher arose in the year 1844, in the southern part of Persia, teaching under the title of The Bab, which term signifies door or gate. He proclaimed the approaching advent of One, a great world teacher, whose divine mission was the uniting in one great spiritual brotherhood of the peoples of all nations, races, and religions, and the establishment of a new spiritual era of oneness of all humanity in spiritual knowledge, and in brotherhood and peace.

The Bab's teaching dwelt upon the coming of the Great Manifestation, of whom He spoke as "He Whom God Would Manifest," exhorting the people to prepare, and purify themselves to meet this Promised One, and to be ready to serve Him when He should appear.

Many seeking souls were attracted by The Bab through His purity and illumination of spirit, for in Him the people not only saw the forerunner of the great universal Messiah, but they realized in Him "The First Point" of the great new age of God in the world.

To The Bab flocked people from the great religions of Persia. Much enthusiasm was manifested by all, and the Mohammedan clergy watched the growth of the movement with jealousy, because they saw thousands of their own people going out from Islam and from the superstitions and forms which they taught. Seeing their own religious hold over the people waning before this teaching, these priests of Islam sought to exterminate the new movement. They incited the fanatical Moslems to pillage, arson, and murder. Thousands of the Babis, followers of The Bab, as they were then called, were massacred, their homes burned, and possessions destroyed; but notwithstanding this persecution the cause continued to grow, the blood of the martyrs being the seed.

The Bab, Himself, was among the first to suffer. Scarcely had His mission begun than He was placed under military surveillance, and after two years of teaching under this difficulty was cast into prison, where He remained for four years, and at the expiration of that time He was tried for heresy before a clerical court, was condemned, and suffered a martyr's death.

Not long after the martyrdom of The Bab, the great world teacher appeared in the person of Baha'o'llah, "He Whom God Manifested." Surrounded by countless fanatical enemies, who strove to destroy Him and His Cause, Baha'o'llah was first known as a leader among the much persecuted Babis; then, later, as His power became manifest to all He was generally acknowledged to be The One Whose Coming The Bab had proclaimed.

From that time on the cause became known as the Bahai Cause, and the followers, as Bahais, while the Babi Cause, as a separate movement, ceased to exist, The Bab's mission and the teaching which He established being not an end in itself but preparatory to the coming of Baha'o'llah.

The Mission of Baha'o'llah lasted forty years, during which time He withstood all manner of trials and persecutions. He was sent out from His home in Persia as an exile and a prisoner to Bagdad in Asiatic Turkey, then to Constantinople in Turkey in Europe, and later to Adrianople in Roumelia, where He remained for five years, afterward enduring, with His family and about seventy followers, men, women, and children, a still more distant exile imprisonment in the fortress of Akka, in the Holy Land. In that country, ever made sacred by God's prophets and Holy Messengers, within view of Mount Carmel, upon which Elijah and others of the prophets had taught, and within a few miles of Nazareth, where Jesus had lived, Baha'o'llah completed the latter half of His active ministrations to humanity.

During the first years of his captivity in Akka, Baha'o'llah and His followers suffered great privations. Confined in the barrack prison under conditions the most unsanitary, illness broke out, and the suffering was so intense that, without the faith and the assurance of soul of all incarcerated, the spirit of the community would have been quite broken, but in reality their persecution and trouble had the effect of increasing their miraculous faith and devotion.

As years passed, the officials of the prison fortress city realized that Baha'o'llah manifested love and harmony, and they became friendly, so, little by little, the condition of the Bahai exiled community was bettered. Baha'o'llah was first given the liberty of the city, and later He was allowed by the governor to reside beyond the walls. The followers from various countries came to receive teachings from Him, returning again to their own lands and peoples fired with the desire to share with others the spiritual pearls of great price which they had found, and thus the cause spread throughout various of the oriental countries.

Baha'o'llah gave His teaching and planted His Cause amid humanity, thus completing His work in this world. Then, for further guidance and development, and for the interpretation and explanation of His teachings, He designated as His successor, His son Abdul Baha.

With the passing from this world of Baha'o'llah, in the late Spring of 1892, began Abdul Baha's mission as the Center of The Bahai Cause. The title of servitude which he chose for himself, namely, "Abdul Baha," means "The Servant of God." Abdul Baha seeks neither honor nor glory for himself other than servant of those who are serving God, yet in the texts of Baha'o'llah the spiritual station of Abdul Baha is clearly set forth as the Center of the Bahai Covenant to humanity.

From his earliest childhood Abdul Baha's life has been devoted to the service of God and humanity. He was with Baha'o'llah during the sixteen years of exile and travel prior to His arrival in Akka, and then began Abdul Baha's long exile of forty years in that fortress, to which the Sultans of Turkey of the old regime used to send their most dreaded enemies, so that its terrible conditions of filth and disease might speedily accomplish their destruction.

It was in August, 1868, that Abdul Baha arrived in Akka with Baha-'o'llah. In August, 1908, when the Turks revolted against former rule, and established a constitutional form of government, Abdul Baha was officially freed; but, during those years of trial, Abdul Baha had accomplished his work, despite the persecution of his enemies, while held, as Baha'o'llah was held, prisoner by the law of Islam because of his progress in teachings. With each added trouble came spiritual growth and strength to the cause. Throughout the years that Abdul Baha was in Akka he labored constantly with his pen, and was able, from time to time, to receive visits from truth seekers of Europe and America, as well as of the near and far East. Now the Bahai Cause is firmly planted in both the Occident and the Orient, and souls are constantly arising to promote Abdul Baha's work.

Some little time after the revolution in Turkey, that brought to Abdul Baha freedom from prison confinement in Akka, he went down into Egypt, and from there visited Paris and London, and later, in the Spring of 1912, he came to these United States, where he spent eight months. He traveled from coast to coast and visited many places where he had friends, and where there were people who wished to hear his explanations of religious questions, and who were desirous of coming into closer touch with that vital illuminating spiritual force which so characterizes his presence.

In America, as well as in England and in France, and, subsequently upon his return to Europe, in both Germany and Austria, the pulpits of Christian churches of many denominations, institutions of learning, and the platforms of philosophical societies and of progressive humanitarian movements of various kinds, sought Abdul Baha, welcomed his message of peace and world oneness, and were rejoiced by the spirit which he radiated.

In his many addresses, most of which have been published, Abdul Baha treats of the creative function of the religion of God, of the great world problems of this present day, and of the solution of these great human difficulties through the application of the true spirit of religion in the lives of the people. Upon all occasions he has taught of the coming of the great world teacher and Manifestation of The Spirit, Baha'o'llah, and of the new spiritual era upon earth that Baha'o'llah inaugurated. Abdul Baha invites all people to approach the Bahai Cause, and for themselves seek and partake of this divine bounty, and to become servants of God and of humanity in carrying this message of the Lord to all peoples.

Those who have seen Abdul Baha, with quickened spiritual eyes of the soul, have realized in him the life-giving spirit of Baha'o'llah, and in Abdul Baha's life of service to humanity the manifested fruit of The Cause of Baha'o'llah.

The Bab was the precursor and "The First Point" of this religious cause in the world today. Baha'o'llah and His teaching formed the root of the movement, which has been compared to a tree, Abdul Baha the branch springing from the root that is Baha'o'llah. As the branch of the tree bears the leaves, flowers, fruits, and seeds, so in the life of Abdul Baha is the world witnessing the budding forth and flowering of the Bahai principles of religion and their application to the needs of humanity.

II.

THE MASHRAK-EL-AZKAR.

Quoted from "Constructive Principles of the Bahai Teachings."

Chapter VIII.

THE MASHRAK-EL-AZKAR.

In every age true religion has produced certain institutions that have served spiritual and practical needs of the people of that time. Such institutions have been a material expression of the spiritual quickening and of the cementing together of the people by the organic, cohesive force of truth. They have naturally grouped themselves about the places of religious worship and meeting, which temples have been the geographic centers of human progress and activity, and the mothers of architecture and the other arts.

Throughout the years of the earliest prophets the people led nomadic lives, going up into the mountains at stated times for their religious observances; thus the open-air altars on the mountains were the recognized religious centers of the collective life of the people.

While the children of Israel were migrating from Egypt to the Holy Land, the tabernacle occupied the central position in their encampment, and later on, in their capital city, Jerusalem, the temple of the Lord crowned the highest hill, and was the center of the intellectual, material, and religious life of the people.

In the typical Christian city of long ago the cathedral has been the great central edifice about which the other buildings of the city, religious and secular, were grouped. The religious life of the people of this epoch was all-important, and this principle was expressed in the architectural development of their cities.

The temple of each religion and civilization is always found to be the focal point of the city architectural. The acropolii of the Greek cities, upon the summits of which were the temples, the forums of the Roman cities, with their many temples, the mosques of the Moslem cities, the fire altars of the Zoroastrians, the pagodas of the Buddhists, and the temples of the Hindus, all testify that each religion has been creative of its own art and civilization in the evolution of an epochal temple.

In times past true religion has been the chief motive force for advancement, learning, and culture. The Bahais now anticipate the day when great universal temples of God will be built, the result of the spiritual quickening of the people, which will signify and further all phases of universal human advancement, spiritual, moral, and physical, of this new age of humanity.

23

The "Mashrak-El-Azkar," which, translated from the Persian, literally means "The Dawning Point of the Mentionings of God," is the Bahai temple of worship and service to humanity. It consists of a central building for worship, the temple proper, surrounded by schools, hospitals and hospices, homes and asylums for the orphan, for the incurable, and for the aged, and by colleges and universities. The temple of the Mashrak-El-Azkar is for reading, meditation, and prayer, not an auditorium for preaching. It is essentially a place for worship and drawing near in spirit to God. Thus it will be a center of spiritual power and attraction, exerting a divine influence in the world.

Its many surrounding institutions are for the practical, moral, and physical service to humanity. The Bahais appreciate that man should glorify God in deed as well as by word of mouth, therefore this principle is embodied in its fullest expression in the Mashrak-El-Azkar.

Some years ago, the first large Mashrak-El-Azkar was built. It is located in the city of Eshkhabad, in Oriental Russia, which has a considerable following of the Bahai Movement, and where the Russian royal government has been friendly to the cause. First, the temple proper was erected, an imposing structure in the oriental style of architecture, and then a school was founded, and a hospice, and now other institutional buildings are being added as the necessary ways and means are available.

Not long past, the friends of the Bahai Movement endeavored to unite in establishing a Mashrak-El-Azkar in America. Contributions were received from the far parts of the world, sent by persons of different countries, races, and religions for the building of this great universal temple, in which peoples of every race and of all religions might find a welcome, and worship there in spirit, and in deed. A very beautiful building site at Chicago, on the shore of Lake Michigan, has been selected and purchased, and it is hoped that sufficient offerings will soon make it possible to begin the work of construction.

When this Mashrak-El-Azkar, with its institutional groups is established, it will be as an ensign to all those who are seeking the great universal spirit of religion, and it will be a practical demonstration of the spirit and of the working principle of service to humanity in the Bahai Cause. Resulting from the united efforts of the friends in its erection, the completed Mashrak-El-Azkar will be a center from which spiritual illumination will radiate, and it will be a haven that will attract seeking and spiritual souls.

III.

THE MASHRAK-EL-AZKAR, OF ESHKHABAD.

Quoted from a letter written in October, 1908, by a Bahai who had traveled in the Orient.

Published in "THE STAR OF THE WEST."

Vol. VI., No. 18.

To the House of Spirituality of Bahais, Chicago, Ill., Brothers in the
Service of Abha:

As you have arisen for the construction of the first Mashrak-El-
Azkar in America, and, as I have recently visited Eshkhabad and seen
there the great Mashrak-El-Azkar of the East, of which we in the West
have heard so much, I take it upon myself to write to you a description
of this edifice, hoping to share with you the great blessing of meeting
with the friends in those parts, and of beholding this temple, which is a
testimony of their sacrifice and unity.

As you know, Eshkhabad is in Russian Turkistan, just north of the
Elbruz mountains, which separate the desert plain of western Turkistan
on the north, from Persia on the south. The city itself lies on the plain
a short distance from the mountains, which here are quite rugged and
rocky. The town is quite modern in aspect, being laid off with gardens
and broad streets meeting at right angles. Rows of trees along the side-
walks remind one of a western city, while the buildings and the waterways, which flank the streets and are fed with water coming from the
nearby mountains, are strikingly oriental.

I could hardly believe that this city had sprung up almost entirely
during the past half century. It was but a huddle of mud huts when
Baha'o'llah first directed some of His followers to settle there. Now this
former village is replaced by a large and prosperous city built of brick
and stone.

The Mashrak-El-Azkar stands in the center of the city, surrounded
by a large garden, which is bounded by four streets. It rises high above
the surrounding buildings and trees, its dome being visible for miles, as
the traveller approaches the city over the plain. The building in plan is
a regular polygon of nine sides. One large doorway and portico, flanked
by turrets, facing the direction of the Holy Land, forms the principal
motive of the façade, while the dome dominates the whole composition.

The walls of the temple are of brick covered with a firm and hard
stucco, which in that climate resists quite well the action of the elements,
while the floors are concrete supported by iron or steel beams.

In plan the building is composed of three sections; namely, the central rotunda, the aisle or ambulatory which surrounds it, and the loggia
which surrounds the entire building.

The interior of the rotunda is five stories in height. The first, or main floor story, consists of nine arches, supported by piers, which separate the ambulatory from the rotunda proper. The second story consists of a similar treatment of arches and piers and balustrades, which separate the triforium gallery, which is directly above the ambulatory, from the wall of the rotunda. The third story is decorated with nine blank arcades, between which are shields, upon which is inscribed, in Persian characters, *"Ya-Baha-el-Abha." The fourth story contains nine large windows, while the wall of the fifth story, which is not as high as the others, is pierced by eighteen bull's-eye windows.

Above, there is the dome which is hemispherical in shape. The rotunda from the floor to the top of the dome is elaborately decorated with fretwork and other designs, all in relief. We were told that the ultimate aim was that color and gilding should be added to this interior decoration.

The inner dome is of iron or steel and concrete, while the outer dome or roof is entirely of metal. The intention is that this shall be gilded.

The main portico of the temple is two stories in the clear, while the loggias, which surround the building, are on two floors, the lower being on the main floor level, while the upper one is on the level of the triforium gallery. This upper loggia is reached by two staircases, one to the right and one to the left of the main entrance, and the gallery is entered from the loggia.

On the main floor the principal entrance is through the large doorway, but there are also several minor doors, which connect the ambulatory with the loggia. An abundance of light is admitted through the windows in the upper part of the rotunda, as well as through the windows of the upper gallery and ambulatory, which open upon the loggias.

The Persian style of architecture has been used in treating the details and decorations of the buildings.

At present the stucco work is not quite completed. The interior of the rotunda is finished, but the decoration of the loggias and gallery and ambulatory is only done in part. However, the work is continuing and it will not be long before all will be complete.

From what I saw and heard in Eshkhabad, I found that those believers who superintended the building of the temple were competent business men and that, although they had undertaken a large enterprise, every possible economy was made, yet at the same time no expense seemed to be spared when necessary for the beauty and solidity of the building.

* "O Thou, The Most Glorious of The Glorious."

The layout of the garden is not yet complete. Nine avenues of approach lead to the Mashrak-El-Azkar. The main avenue of the nine, leading to the entrance portico, will be entered from the street by a monumental gateway. Last July they were completing the plans for this principal gateway of the grounds.

At the four corners of the garden are four buildings. One is a school, one is a house where traveling Bahais are entertained, one is to be used as a hospital, and the other is for workmen, storage, etc. Much of the property in the immediate vicinity of this enclosure belongs to Bahais, so the Mashrak-El-Azkar is the center of the community materially, as well as spiritually.

That which impressed me more than all else, as I stood before this Mashrak-El-Azkar, was the fact that the Bahais of the East had all worked with one accord and had given freely toward its erection.

The temple in America can be accomplished only as we give up self and unite in this service. The beloved in the East made their offerings and left them with all personal desires upon the altar of sacrifice. Now we in this country must do likewise! We need something more than money for the Mashrak-El-Azkar. It must be built of the material of sacrifice and cemented together by the spirit of unity.

In the building of the Mashrak-El-Azkar every one should lay before God his material offering together with his ideas, desires, and aspirations, give them to the Lord completely, and then, as we come together to construct the material building we will find that we have ample means both spiritual and material for the work in hand.

Each one of us has sufficient means for the work which God has given us to perform. We need not trouble thinking that we may not have enough means, but rather we should seek to apply to the best advantage the means which God has given us.

IV.

WORDS OF ABDUL BAHA REGARDING THE MASHRAK-EL-AZKAR IN AMERICA.

Compiled from articles published in "THE STAR OF THE WEST."

Vol. V., No. 5, and Vol. VI., No. 17, and in the program pamphlet of the eighth annual Mashrak-El-Azkar convention.

WORDS OF ABDUL BAHA.

I send you the glad tidings of the erection of the Mashrak-El-Azkar, the Bahai Temple, in Eshkhabad, with all joy and great happiness. The friends of God assembled together with rejoicing, and conveyed the stones themselves upon their backs, while attracted by the love of God, and for the glory of God. Soon that great temple will be completed and the voice of prayer and praise shall ascend to the Sublime Kingdom.

I was rejoiced through your endeavors in this glorious cause, made with joy and good interest. I pray God to aid you in exalting His Word, and in establishing the temple of worship, through His grace and ancient mercy. Verily, ye are the first to arise for this glorious cause in that vast region. Soon will ye see the spread of this enterprise in the world, and its resounding voice shall go through the ears of the people in all parts.

Exert your energy in accomplishing what ye have undertaken, so that this glorious temple may be built, that the beloved of God may assemble therein, and that they may pray and offer glory to God for guiding them to His Kingdom.

Now the day has arrived in which the edifice of God, the divine sanctuary, the spiritual temple, shall be erected in America. I entreat God to assist the confirmed believers in accomplishing this great service, and with entire zeal to rear this mighty structure, which shall be renowned throughout the world. The support of God will be with those believers in that district, that they may be successful in their undertaking. For the cause is great, because this is the first Mashrak-El-Azkar in that country, and from it the praise of God shall ascend to the Kingdom of Mystery, and the tumult of His exaltation and greeting from the whole world shall be heard.

Whosoever arises for the service of this building shall be assisted with great power from His Supreme Kingdom, and upon him spiritual and heavenly blessings shall descend, which shall fill his heart with wonderful consolation and enlighten his eyes by beholding the Glorious and Eternal God.

* * * * * * *

When the Mashrak-El-Azkar is accomplished, when the lights are emanating therefrom, the righteous ones are presenting themselves therein, the prayers are performed with supplication towards the mysterious Kingdom of Heaven, the voice of glorification is raised to the Lord, the Supreme; then the believers shall rejoice, and the hearts shall be dilated and overflowed with the love of the All-Living and Self-Existent God.

The people shall hasten to worship in that heavenly temple, the fragrances of God will be elevated, and the divine teachings will be established in the hearts like the establishment of the spirit in mankind. The people will then stand firm in the cause of your Lord, the Merciful.

*   *   *   *   *   *   *

To have the Mashrak-El-Azkar built is most important. Some material things have spiritual effect, and the Mashrak-El-Azkar is a material thing that will have great effect upon the spirits of the people. Not only does the building of the Mashrak-El-Azkar have an effect upon those who build it, but upon the whole world.

*   *   *   *   *   *   *

The Mashrak-El-Azkar, though outwardly a material foundation, is possessed of spiritual effect and causes the union of hearts and the gathering of souls.

In the days of the Manifestation (prophet) any city wherein a temple was founded afforded the means of promulgation of the cause, and the confirmation of the hearts and the confidence of souls, for in those dwellings the Name of God is ever mentioned and always commemorated, and, for the tranquility and repose of the hearts, there is no other means save the commemoration of Almighty God.

Praise be to God! The erection of the Mashrak-El-Azkar has a great effect in all grades, or states. It was tested in the East, and so, evidently and plainly, was it proved. Even when in a village a house was called the Mashrak-El-Azkar it possessed a different effect. How much more its building and organization!

Therefore, O ye friends and maid-servants of the Merciful! As long as ye can, endeavor with life and heart, so that the Mashrak-El-Azkar of Chicago may soon be built, organized, and confirmed.

If all the friends in America, in all cities and hamlets, assist, and by the means of a building commission help, this offering will prove most acceptable in the Kingdom of the Sun of the Horizons.

*   *   *   *   *   *   *

Among the most important affairs is the founding of the Mashrak-El-Azkar, although weak minds may not grasp its importance; nay, perchance, they imagine this Mashrak-El-Azkar to be a temple like other temples.

34

They may say to themselves: "Every nation has a hundred thousand gigantic temples. What result have they yielded, that now this one Mashrak-El-Azkar is said to cause the manifestation of signs and prove a source of light?" They are ignorant of the fact that the founding of this Mashrak-El-Azkar is to be in the inception of the organization of the Kingdom.

Therefore, it is important and is an expression of the uprising of the Evident Standard, which is waving in the center of that continent, the results and effects of which will become manifest in the hearts and spirits. No soul will be aware of this mature wisdom save after trial.

When the Mashrak-El-Azkar was founded in Eshkhabad, its clamor affected all the cities of the Orient and caused souls to awaken to the call. Most of the souls who investigated and heard the explanation were attracted to the Kingdom of God.

*　　*　　*　　*　　*　　*　　*

The greatest interrelation and communication exists between the sons of men, without which peace, life, and existence are entirely impossible. For a soul independent of all the other souls, and without receiving assistance from other sources, cannot live for the twinkling of an eye; nay, rather, he will become non-existent and reduced to nothingness, especially among the believers of God, between whom material and spiritual communication is developed up to the highest point of perfection.

It is this real communication, the essential necessity and requirement of which is mutual helpfulness, cöoperation, and confirmation. Without the complete establishment of this divine principle in the hearts of the friends of God nothing can be accomplished, for they are the hyacinths of one garden, the waves of one sea, the stars of one heaven, and the rays of one sun. From every standpoint the essential unity, the luminous unity, the religious unity, and the material unity are founded and organized between them.

In these times the utmost hope and wish of the friends of the West is the erection of the Mashrak-El-Azkar, and in those regions the materials for construction and building are expensive and costly. A large sum of money is needed for the building of a residence, then how much more is needed for the foundation of the Mashrak-El-Azkar, which must be erected with the utmost splendor, beauty, and magnificence!

Therefore, the friends of God must arise in every part of the world to raise contributions, and with their hearts and souls strive to gather these funds to be sent to the Occident, that it may become known and evident throughout the universe that the Bahais of the East and West are as members of one household, and the children of the one Lord! The Turks and the Persians, the Parsee and the American, the Hindu and the African; all of them are one army and one cohort, and without any distinction they arise for the assistance and aid of each other.

This praiseworthy movement is beloved and accepted at the threshold of the forgiving Lord. Truly, I say, in the erection of the Mashrak-El-Azkar in Eshkhabad the friends of God have laid the foundation of the oneness of the kingdom of humanity, and they worked nobly together until now, and it is nearly completed. Praise be to God, that, at this moment, from every country in the world, according to their various means, contributions are continually being sent toward the fund of the Mashrak-El-Azkar in America.

In reality, this magnanimity of the believers is worthy of great praise and thankfulness; for, from Teheran, Khorossan, Shiraz, Jahram, Esphahan, even from the towns and villages of Khorassan, Shiraz, and Yazd contributions were sent. This donation in the path of the Orb of Regions is conducive to the happiness of the souls of the spiritual ones.

From the day of Adam until now such an event has never even been witnessed by man; that, from the farthermost country of Asia, contributions were forwarded to the farthermost country of America. From Rangoon, India, donations are sent to Chicago, and from Jahram, a little village of Shiraz, and Kheirol-Gora of Tarshiz, money is transmitted for the Mashrak-El-Azkar in America. This is through the bounty and providence of the Blessed Perfection, the assistance and confirmation of the Sun of Truth, and the victory and triumph of the Luminary of Effulgence, who has united so marvelously the regions of the world together. Glory belongs to the Lord of Hosts. Sovereignty belongs to the compassionate God. Power and might belong to the living, Selfsubsistent One, who has united the people of the world and assembled them together like unto the brilliant stars of the horizon of adoration.

*   *   *   *   *   *   *

The accessories of the Mashrak-El-Azkar are numerous. Among them are the school for orphans, the great college for the higher arts, hospital, and home for the cripples and hospice. The doors of these places are to be opened to all sects—no differentiations. When these accessories are completed, and, by God's help and aid, the departments fully systematized, it will be proved that the Mashrak-El-Azkar is to human society a great bounty and a great blessing.

In brief, through the unlimited bounties of God I am hopeful that the beloved ones of God in America may be aided and confirmed in founding this mighty and solid foundation, and gradually annex thereto its accessories.

* * * * * * *

When these institutions, college, hospital, hospice and establishments for the incurables, university for the study of higher sciences, giving post-graduate courses, and other philanthropic buildings are built their doors will be opened to all the nations and religions. There will be absolutely no line of demarcation drawn. Its charities will be dispensed irrespective of color or race. Its gates will be flung wide open to mankind; prejudice toward none, love for all. The central building will be devoted to the purpose of prayer and worship. Thus, for the first time, religion will become harmonized with science, and science will be the handmaid of religion, both showering their material and spiritual gifts on all humanity."

* * * * * * *

ADDRESS OF ABDUL BAHA AT THE DEDICATION OF THE MASHRAK-EL-AZKAR GROUNDS.

Chicago, High Noon, May 1, 1912.

Today you have endured considerable difficulty in coming out, withstanding the cold and wind, but the power which has gathered you here is truly a colossal power. It is the extraordinary power. It is a divine power which gathers you here. It is the divine favor of Baha'o'llah which gathered you together. Therefore, we praise God that this power does assemble people in this fashion.

Thousands of Mashrak-El-Azkars, which mean the Dawning Points of Praise for all religionists, will be built in the world. In the Orient and in the Occident of the world will they be built, but this Mashrak-El-Azkar, being the first one in the Occident, has great importance. In after years there will be many Mashrak-El-Azkars; even in this city of Chicago many will be established. In Asia there will be many. In Europe there will be many. Even in Africa there will be many. Even in Australia and New Zealand, but this one in America is of great importance. In Eshkhabad, Russia, the Mashrak-El-Azkar has the same great importance, being the first one built there. In Persia there are many Mashrak-El-Azkars. Some are houses, which have been rented for that purpose. Others have given their homes entirely for that purpose, and in some places temporary and small places have been built therefor. In all the cities of Persia there are Mashrak-El-Azkars, but the great Mashrak-El-Azkar was founded in Eshkhabad. Because it was the first Mashrak-El-Azkar it possesses the superlative degree of importance. All the friends of Esh-khabad agreed and put forth the greatest effort. His holiness the Afnan* devoted all his wealth to it. Everything he had he gave for it. Hence, such an imposing edifice was built. A colossal effort was put forth. Notwithstanding their contributions to that Mashrak-El-Azkar they have, as you know, contributed to the one here in this city. Now that one is almost complete; that is to say, with all its gardens. That Mashrak-El-Azkar is centrally located. It has nine avenues, nine gardens, nine fountains, so it is nine on nine, all nines. It is like a beautiful bouquet. Just imagine an edifice of that beauty in the center, very lofty, surrounded by gardens, variegated flowers, with nine avenues interlacing nine gardens, nine pools, and nine fountains, and think how delightful it must be! That is the way it should be. It is matchless, most beautiful! Such is the design, and now they are at work building a hospital and a school for orphans, and a home for cripples, and a large dispensary and a hospice. They are now planning, thinking of these things. When that, God willing, shall be completed, it will be a Paradise! There will be no greater geometry than this, and I hope that in Chicago it shall be like this. It will be even so.

---

* A Relative of The Bab.

V.

THE SITE FOR THE FIRST MASHRAK-EL-AZKAR IN AMERICA.

THE SITE FOR THE FIRST MASHRAK-EL-AZKAR IN AMERICA.

The site for the Mashrak-El-Azkar, now free from all encumbrances, is in the borough of Wilmette, Chicago, bordering on Lake Michigan.

Compared with the flat character of the surrounding country the Mashrak-El-Azkar land is high, affording a commanding view of the lake. This tract of about nine acres is divided into two unequal parts by Sheridan Road, which is the lake-side boulevard connecting Chicago and Milwaukee. It is planned to build the temple proper of the Mashrak-El-Azkar upon the larger of the two tracts, which measures about six acres and lies to the west of Sheridan Road, which here runs north and south, while the smaller tract, of about three acres, extending east from the road down to the lake shore is to be improved and laid out as a park, thus giving an approach by water to the Mashrak-El-Azkar with its grounds.

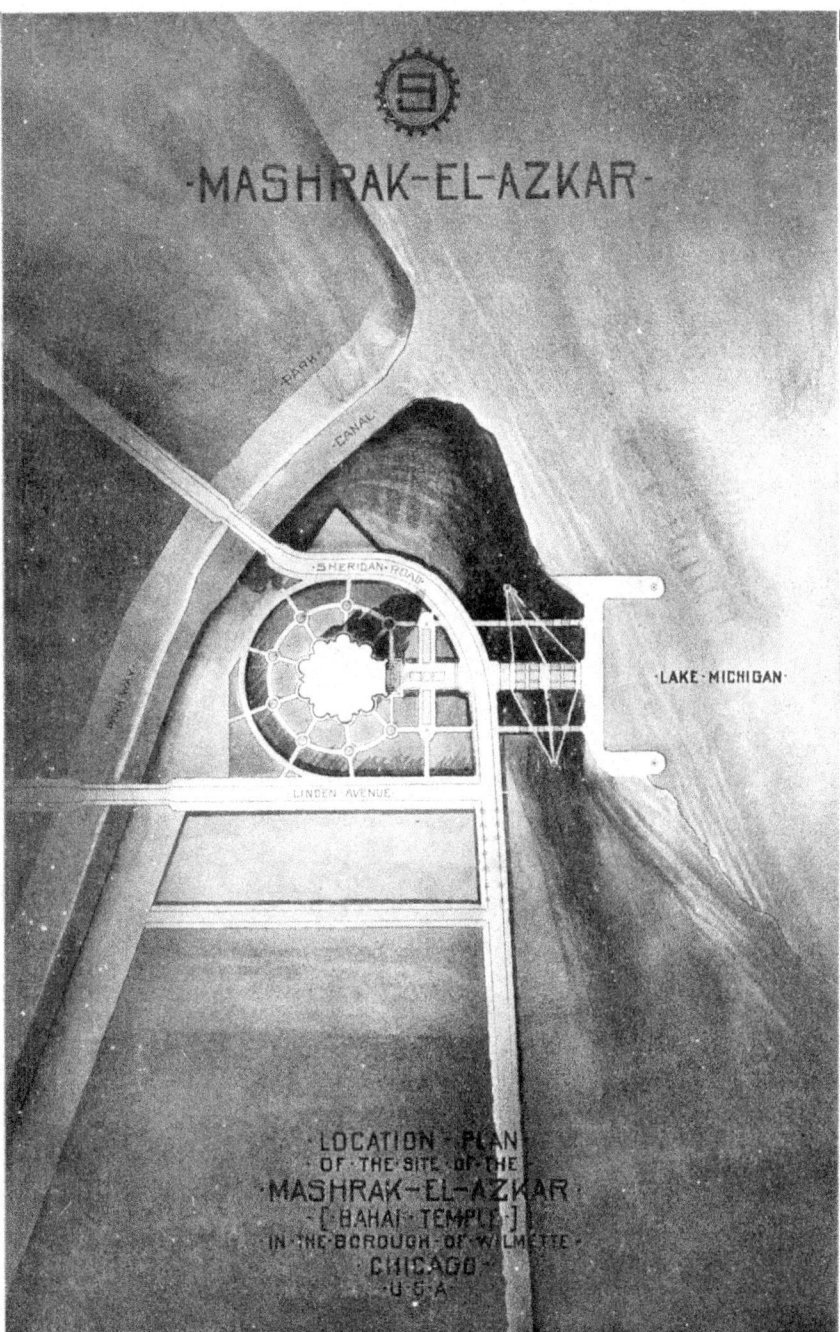

·MASHRAK–EL–AZKAR·

·LAKE·MICHIGAN·

·LOCATION·PLAN·
·OF·THE·SITE·OF·THE·
·MASHRAK–EL–AZKAR·
·[·BAHAI·TEMPLE·]·
·IN·THE·BOROUGH·OF·WILMETTE·
·CHICAGO·
·U·S·A·

VI.

THE ARCHITECTURAL PROBLEM.

Its requirements and conditions.

ARCHITECTURAL PROBLEM.

The temple proper of The Mashrak-El-Azkar will eventually be the central feature of a group of buildings housing auxiliary, philanthropic, and charitable institutions which will be erected as the ways and means are available, all of which taken together form the Mashrak-El-Azkar; however, for the present the architectural problem may be considered to be confined to the one main edifice, the temple, the entire site so far acquired being intended exclusively for this one building with its parks, gardens, and approaches.

In general, the requirements of the temple of the Mashrak-El-Azkar are: that it should be built upon the plan of a polygon of nine sides, that it should be surmounted by a dome, that the interior rotunda with encircling galleries should be supported by nine piers, that the building should have one principal portal facing the east, and that the edifice should be surrounded by a park divided into nine gardens, each with a fountain, by nine avenues radiating from the building. Beyond these simple general conditions no authoritative data has as yet been given out.

In making the following designs the architect has tried to vary the different treatments to present a number of motives and compositions, in order to show some of the many varying architectural solutions applicable to this problem of a Mashrak-El-Azkar.

VII.

STYLES OF ARCHITECTURE AND DESCRIPTIONS OF DESIGNS.

GENERAL DESCRIPTION.

STYLES. Preceding each of the following designs for the Mash-rak-El-Azkar is a brief outline of the history and character of the style of architecture in which the problem is conceived.

DRAWINGS. Each of these designs comprises a set of four drawings, showing in elevation, plans, and section the arrangement of the building with its various parts as described in the text.

THE EAST ELEVATION shows the general exterior architectural treatment with the main portal and its approach.

THE GENERAL PLAN shows the arrangement of the main floor of the building, together with the surrounding terraces, gardens, fountains, walks, drives, and other approaches.

THE ROOF PLAN shows a horizontal section taken through the upper part, looking down upon the lower part of the building.

In design 2 a plan of the foundations and crypt has been shown in place of a roof plan.

THE SECTION taken vertically east and west through the center of the building shows the interior arrangement of the entrance, portico, rotunda, ambulatory, crypt, domes, vaults, and galleries, with minor staircases and elevators built in the thicknesses of the walls, which connect the different floor levels of the building.

NOTE.

In designs 1, 3, 5, 6, and 7 a development has been given to the east bay of the building in order to accentuate the main portal.

This has been accomplished in the following way: A circle was described and divided into nineteen equal sectors. The area of three of these was taken for the development of the east bay of the building, thus having the area of two sectors for the development of each of the other eight bays.

With the exception of design 9, which is symmetrical as viewed from any of its faces, each of the designs calls for a projection of the eastern bay in order to accommodate in plan the main portal, or vestibule.

51

DESIGN NO. 1.

ROMAN CLASSIC STYLE OF ARCHITECTURE.

THE ROMAN CLASSIC STYLE OF ARCHITECTURE, product of the civilization of ancient Rome, the fundamental elements of which the Romans borrowed from the Greeks and earlier peoples, is exemplified in the many Roman remains extant in various parts of Europe and northern Africa. Some Roman ruins of vast proportions are found as far east as Baalbek and Palmyra in Syria.

Roman architecture covered a very broad field, including buildings religious and secular. The forums of cities with their temples, tombs, theatres, amphitheatres, baths, palaces, basilicas, gateways, triumphal arches, bridges, and aqueducts were richly embellished, to the point ·of luxury.

The Roman style, with modifications adapts itself readily to certain of the big architectural problems of this present day. "The Pantheon" and the "Church of the Madeleine" in Paris, as well as many other edifices in the various European cities, the Capitol at Washington, and a number of State Houses and other public buildings in America, are successful applications of the Roman classic to suit modern conditions.

The decorative possibilities of this style are varied. Marbles of various colors, mosaics, painting, and sculpture are equally applicable and in character.

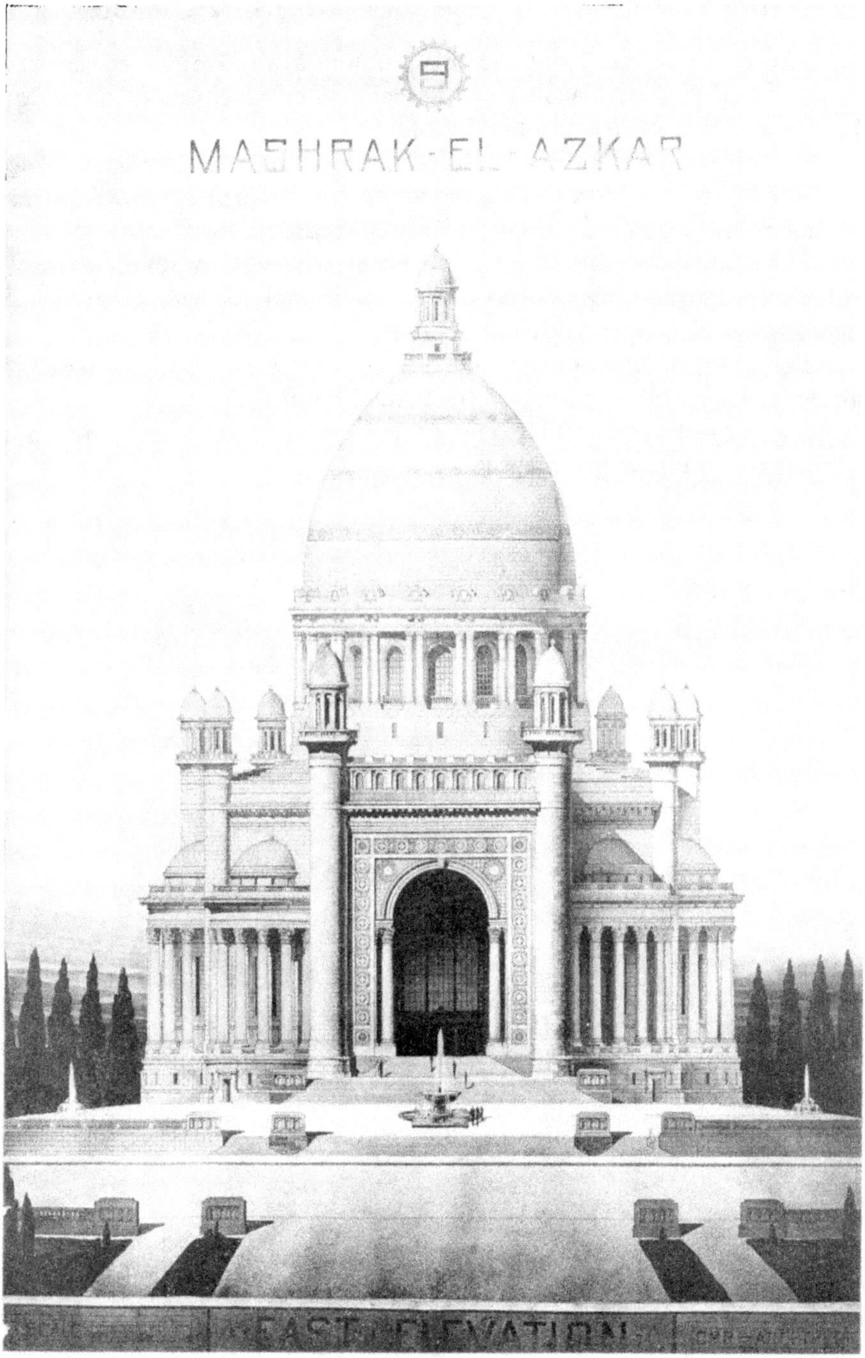

MAṢHRAK-EL-AZKAR

The architect has imagined this building in the Roman classic style, to be constructed of masonry with steel reinforcements and supports in the construction of the dome and roofs.

The exterior walls, turrets, dome, and roof are of light toned granite.

The interior is finished in stone and colored marbles, with scultpured ornament and frescoes. The floors are of mosaic.

The arches of the rotunda support two superimposed stories of galleries. Surrounding the rotunda on the main floor level is an ambulatory, from which open eight large apses.

The exterior is dominated by the dome, while at each corner of the building is a turret surmounted by a small dome. From the faces of the building project semicircular bays roofed by half domes and surrounded by colonnades forming the apses.

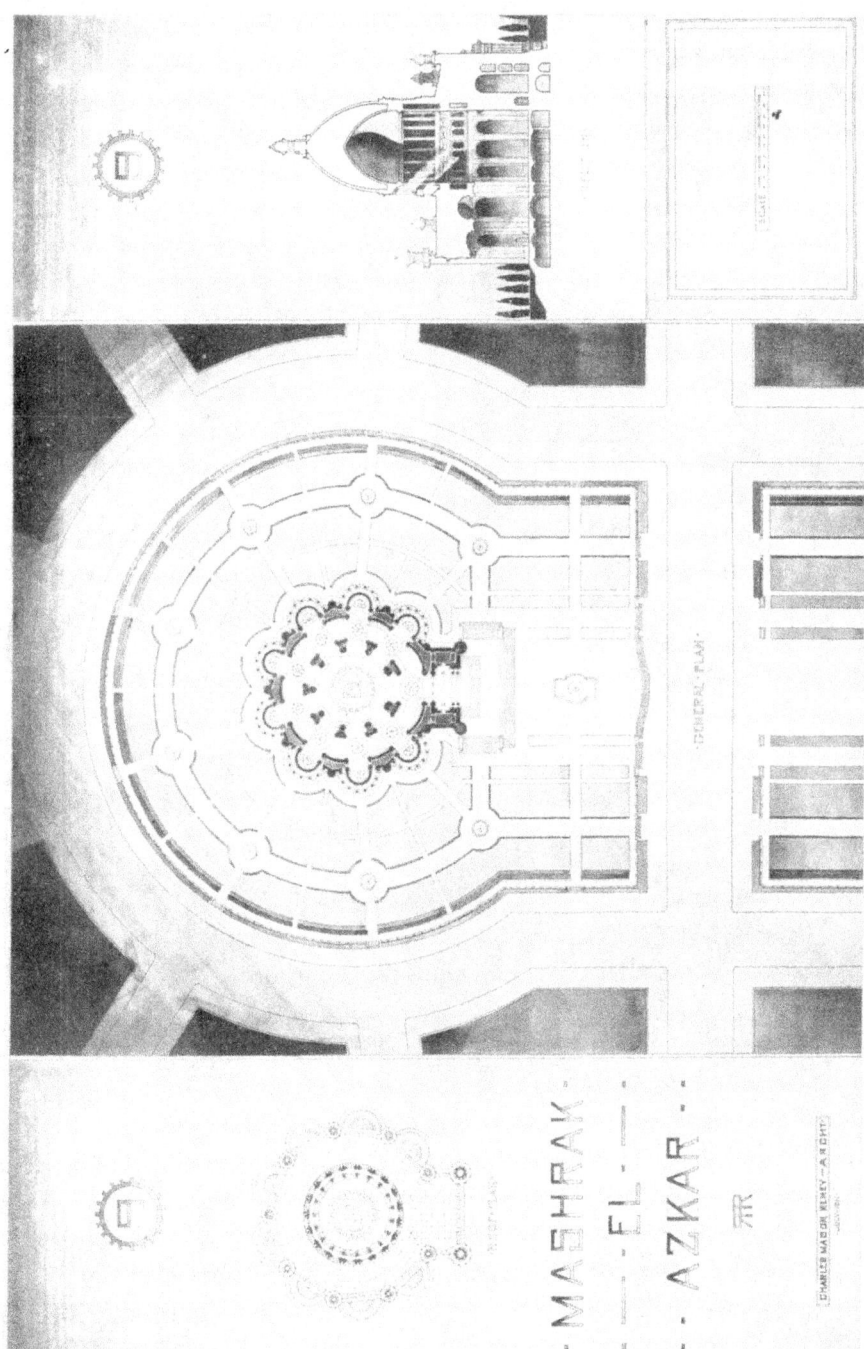

· MASHRAK ·
· — · EL · — ·
· · AZKAR · ·

· GENERAL · PLAN ·

CHARLES MASON REMEY — ARCHT.

59

DESIGN NO. 2.

BYZANTINE STYLE OF ARCHITECTURE.

THE BYZANTINE STYLE OF ARCHITECTURE followed the classic period, and was the first matured style of Christian architecture. Attaining its finest development in the Sixth century, it flourished in Turkey, Greece, and Syria, while some examples of the epoch are found as far east as Armenia, and others on the west in Italy. The Byzantine of southern France is of a somewhat later date.

The mosque of "Santa Sophia," originally a Christian church at Constantinople, is without doubt the most beautiful, famous, and admired example of Byzantine, while "S. Vitalae," at Ravenna, and "St. Marks," at Venice, as well as the cathedral of "St. Front" at Perigeux in southern France—these latter two of the 11th century—are fine examples of the application of this style.

Among the successful and well-known examples of the adaptation of Byzantine to modern buildings for worship are the cathedrals of Westminster and of Marseilles, and the recently completed basilica of the "Sacred Heart" on the Butte of Montmartre in Paris. This latter, though decoratively less florid than some other examples of the style, like those of the earlier French Byzantine, produces nevertheless an effect of impressive dignity which cannot be questioned.

The Byzantine, though massive in construction, calls in its most complete development for sculptured ornament, and interior decorations of marble and mosaic, rich in color, which relieve it from any seeming structural heaviness.

The architect has imagined this building in the Byzantine style, to be constructed entirely of masonry.

The exterior is of light granite, including the domes as well as the roofs, which are formed of slabs supported by the interior vaulting.

The interior, of stone and marble, relieved by sculptured ornament and richly decorated with mosaics, is entered through a high arched portico. Upon either side of the vestibule are staircases leading to the crypt below, which is so designed as to serve for religious purposes, supplementing the main part of the building. In a sub-crypt below the vestibule provision has been made for a vault for the storage of records and archives.

The rotunda, entered from the vestibule, is encircled by piers and arches which support two stories of galleries. Surrounding the rotunda on the main floor level, is an ambulatory, from which opens out a series of apses.

The exterior of the building is dominated by the great dome, which surmounts the central rotunda, about the base of which rise nine small domes which are above the ambulatory. From the faces of the building project the semicircular walls forming the apses of the interior, and upon the exterior these are encircled by semicircular arcaded porticoes, to which there is access from the interior. Above these portions are open balconies upon a level with and entered from the galleries. A semicircular retaining wall, with a colonnade supporting a terrace above on the level of the main gardens, is arranged in the rear of the building, with staircases connecting the levels.

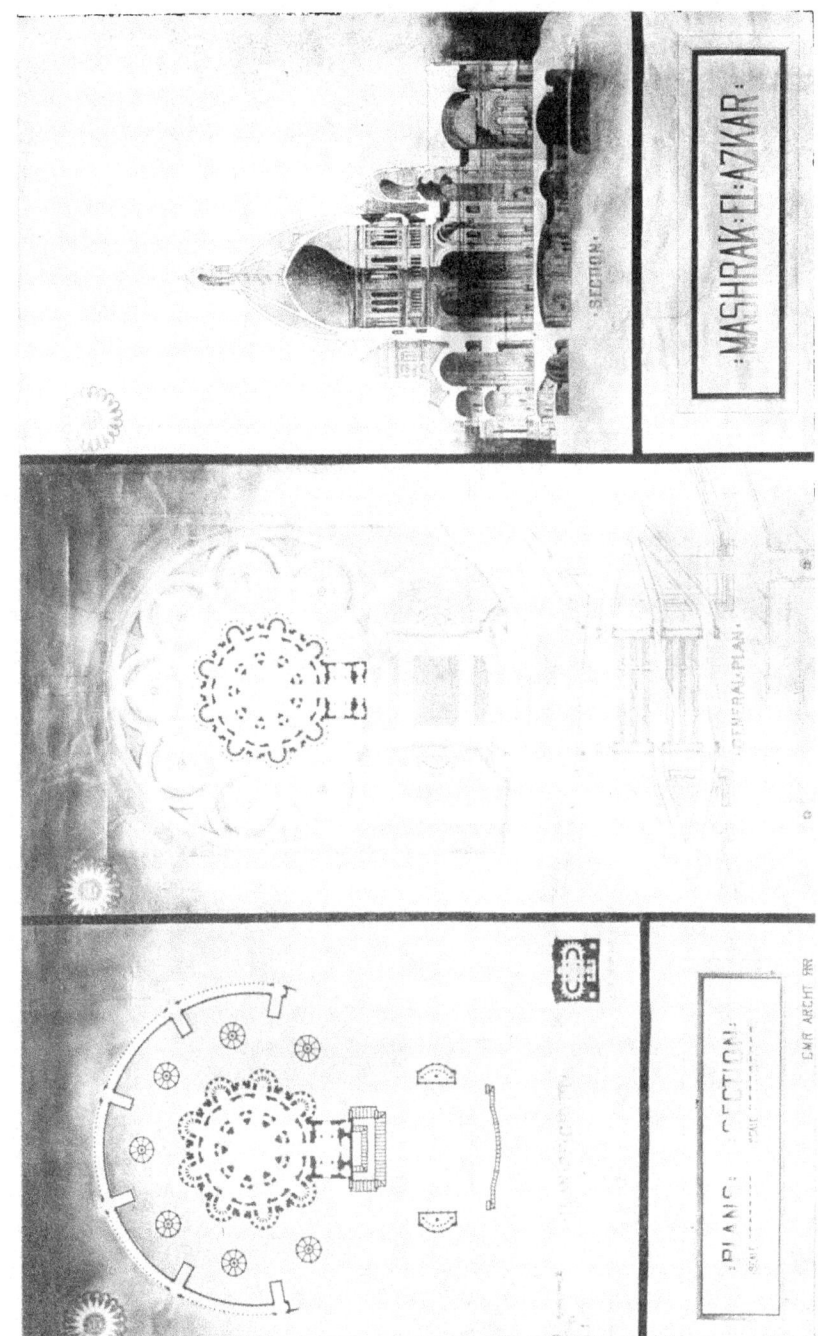

DESIGN NO. 3.

ARABIAN-MOORISH STYLE OF ARCHITECTURE.

THE ARABIAN AND MOORISH STYLES of architecture were evolved by the Moslem civilization, reaching their perfection, respectively, in northern Africa and in Spain.

The palace of the Alhambra at Grenada, and the great mosque at Cordova, now transformed and used as a cathedral, are the finest and best known examples of Moorish art.

The mosques of Cairo represent the finest examples of pure Arabian architecture, while many tombs and houses of Cairo testify to the beauty of the Arabian period.

The Arabian buildings attained a grandeur of size, general proportions, and composition not reached in the Moorish style, yet the Moors attained an elegance and a refinement in decoration which is not found in Arabian art. The architectural and decorative elements of these two styles can be used together in harmonious composition.

The decoration of the Arabian and Moorish buildings is carried out in marbles, colored tiles, and very elaborate fretwork designs in colors and gold, producing an effect gorgeous, but at the same time dignified and harmonious. The horseshoe arch is one of the most striking features of these styles.

MASHRAK-EL-AZKAR

The architect has imagined this building in the Arabian-Moorish style to be of masonry, with steel reinforcements and supports in the construction of the dome and roof.

The exterior wall surfaces, dome, roof, and retaining walls of surrounding terraces are of white sandstone.

The interior is finished in stone and colored marbles, with sculptural and plastic ornament in gold and colors.

The building is entered by a vestibule portal, upon either side of which are staircases leading to the loggias upon the floor above.

The rotunda is encircled by nine arches, which support a gallery of nineteen bays, and the dome above is pierced by an equal number of star-shaped openings. Surrounding the rotunda is a narrow aisle or ambulatory, and then a second one of more ample dimensions, above which is a spacious gallery giving upon a series of loggias which overlook the terraces and gardens.

The exterior of the building in general lines is extremely simple, with decoration in low though crisp relief. The most striking feature of the main façade is the high triple arched portal. The entire building rests upon a high terrace surrounded by retaining walls and abutments with stair approaches. Fountains are set into large grotto niches in the terrace-retaining wall, and from these fountains radiate avenues and gardens.

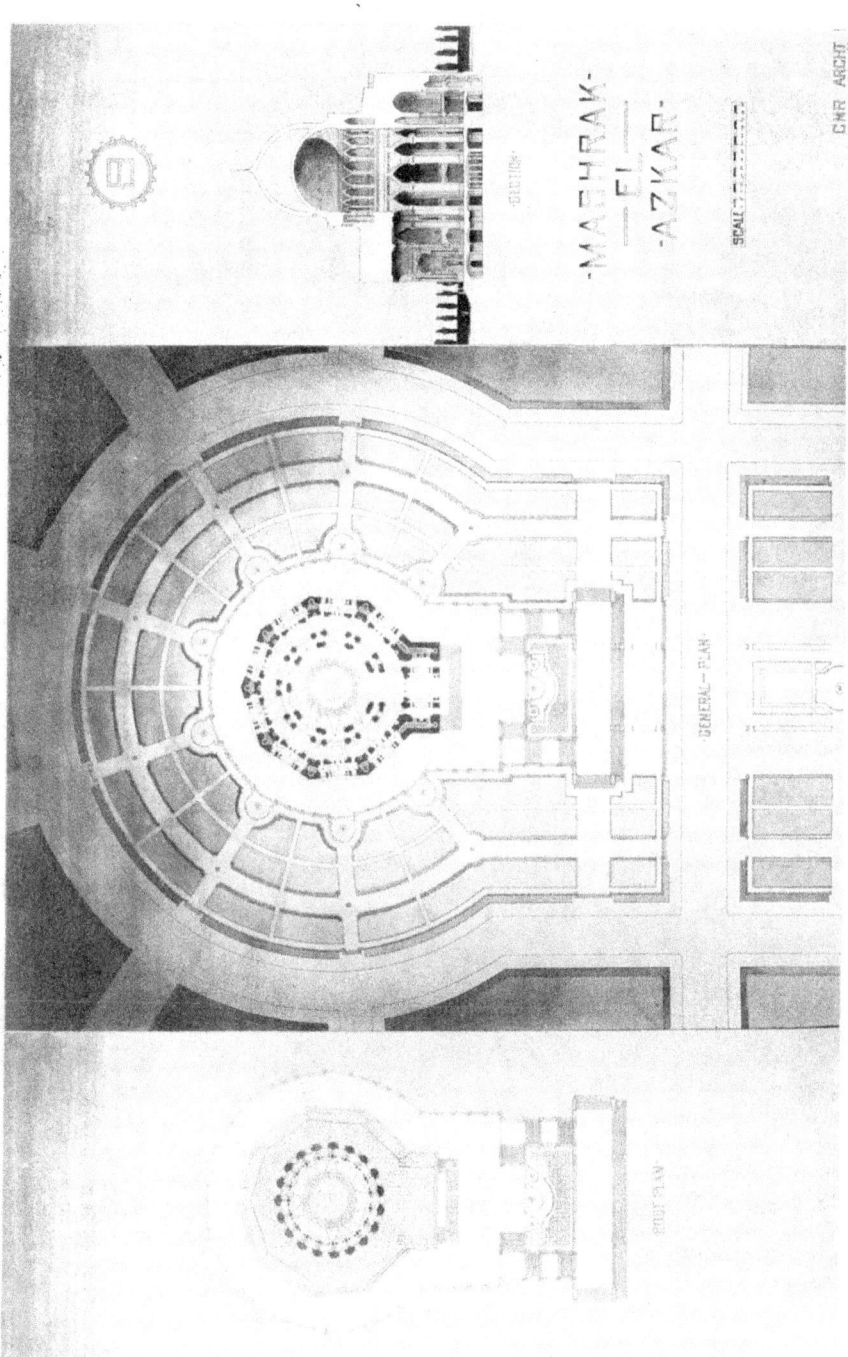

-MASHRAK-
-EL-
-AZKAR-

·SECTION·

SPALE·····

·GENERAL·PLAN·

·ROOF·PLAN·

CWR ARCHT

75

DESIGN NO. 4.

PERSIAN STYLE OF ARCHITECTURE.

THE PERSIAN STYLE OF ARCHITECTURE was developed under the influence brought into Persia by the early Moslem civilization. Some of its grandest applications are found in the mosques of Esphahan, Khoum, Kashan, and Khazvin, while the same style is found in those and other cities, successfully applied to such buildings as bazaars, caravansaries, palaces, colleges, gateways, bridges, and other civic structures.

The lower wall surfaces of the more elegant of these buildings are often revetted with slabs of marble, while the main walls and upper parts are usually in brick, terra cotta, and brightly colored tiles. Though some of these buildings have stood for centuries, the coloring in many instances remains quite fresh and even brilliant.

The richness in color decoration of the domes and minarets of Persian mosques, rising from a foreground of gardens and silhouetted against a cloudless sky, is very memorable and beautiful. This style of decoration, so in harmony with its oriental environment, has a charm of its own, to which many Persian writers, as well as foreigners traveling in that country, have testified.

MASHRAK EL AZKAR

The architect has imagined this building in the Persian style to be of a masonry construction of concrete and brick faced with colored tiles and terra cotta.

The exterior is finished with tiles and terra cotta, and the lower parts faced with slabs of colored marbles.

The interior is finished in materials similar to those utilized upon the exterior, to which is added mosaic. A high rotunda with galleries forms the central motive of the composition of the interior.

About the central rotunda is a series of nine smaller rotundas, while upon the main floor a loggia passageway encircles the entire building, uniting the main portico with each of the minor porticoes.

The exterior of the building is so proportioned that the dome rises high above the other parts of the building, so that it will dominate the landscape. Each façade contains three large and spacious niches, which form the loggia porticoes through which the building is entered.

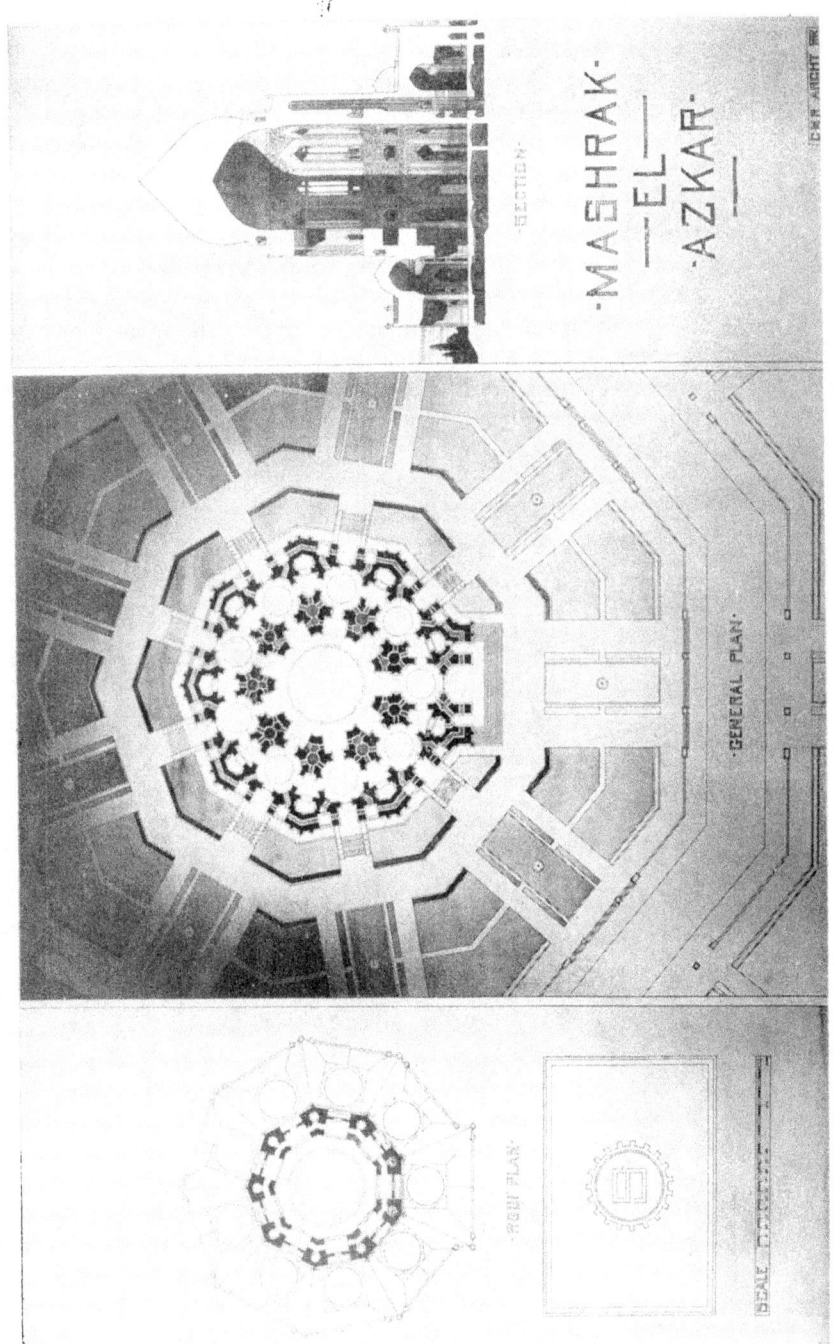

·MASHRAK· —— ·EL· —— ·AZKAR·

·SECTION·

·GENERAL PLAN·

·ROOF PLAN·

·SCALE·

DESIGN NO. 5.

INDIAN STYLE OF ARCHITECTURE.

THE INDIAN STYLE OF ARCHITECTURE had its richest development during the Mogul rule in India. In this civilization art and architecture show a strong Persian influence. Some of the finest examples of this style are found in the vicinity of Delhi, India's ancient capital, while the world-famous Taj-Mahal, near the city of Agra, though not so pure in details as other mosques of the period, nevertheless is without doubt the best known and by many the most admired building of the epoch.

The Taj-Mahal is finished within and without with white marble inlaid with jasper, lapis lazuli, and other semi-precious stones. It is surrounded by a garden intersected by waterways separated by richly colored flowers and foliage, and produces an effect of beauty beyond the power of words to describe.

The architect has imagined this building in the Indian Style to be constructed of masonry, with the exception of the inner and outer shells of the dome, which require steel reinforcing. Both the exterior and the interior would be finished in white marble, in the latter to be relieved here and there by inlays of colored marbles, and decorated with sculptured ornament.

In conceiving this design the architect has in mind a structure much less in dimensions than others here illustrated. It will be seen from the drawings, therefore, that both the exterior and interior arrangements are simple in the extreme.

The rotunda is encircled by nine columns, which support a gallery of nineteen bays. Upon the main floor the central space is surrounded by deep windowed alcoves, which are connected by passageways piercing the walls behind the columns, while above is a gallery story similarly treated. Upon either side of the main entrance are staircases leading to the galleries.

The dome is the most striking feature of the exterior. Engaged with the building at each corner are minaret turrets terminating in miniature domes. The interior arrangement of main and gallery floors is indicated on the exterior by the two stories of windows.

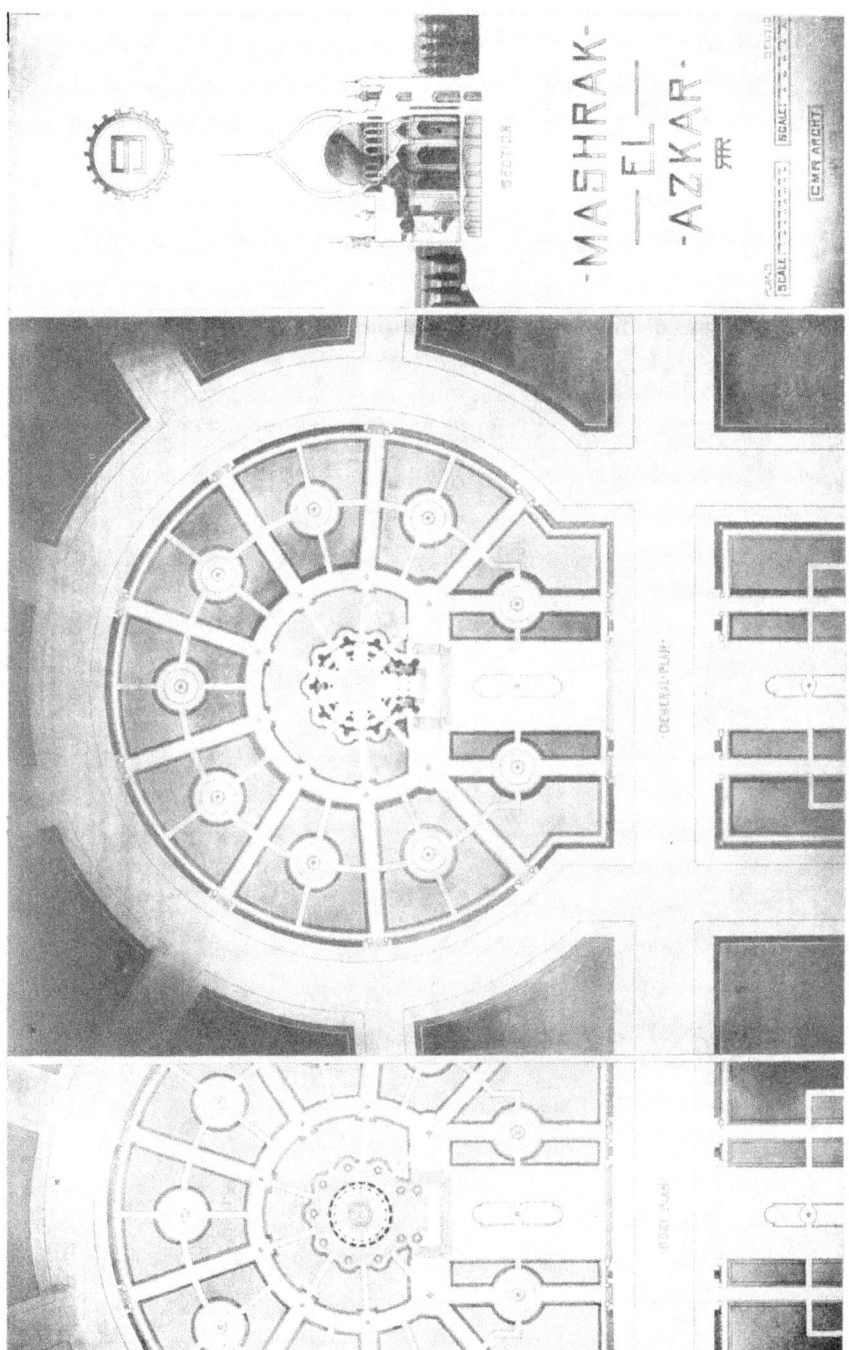

DESIGN NO. 6.

ROMANESQUE STYLE OF ARCHITECTURE.

THE ROMANESQUE STYLE OF ARCHITECTURE is peculiar to the buildings of the period which was transitional between the Roman and the Gothic epochs.

As with all transitional periods of art, the examples of the Romanesque are most varied, and exhibit the influence of the inventiveness and the traditions, and the culture of the people in the several European countries, as well as in the few near eastern lands in which its monuments are found, its development extending over an age of constructive ingenuity beginning with the late and decadent classic, and leading up to the most highly structurally developed of all styles yet evolved—the Gothic.

In its earliest stages the Romanesque still retains much of the classic, and in some of the countries where abounded buildings and remains of the classic period the traditions of the people were such that it was never freed from this influence, while in its latter stages of evolution, notably exemplified in the churches of northern France, are to be found elements which exhibit in rudiment the principles of the Gothic structural system.

The monuments of this epoch are very widespread. Some fine examples of the Romanesque development are found in Auvergne in south central France, of which the church of "Notre-Dame-du-Port," at Clermont-Ferrand, is one of the best examples. The churches in northern France, in particular the abbys of Caen and the church of "St. Etienne," at Beauvais, show important developments in the evolution of the style.

In Germany the cathedrals of Mayence, Speyer, and Worms are grand examples of the character of the Romanesque peculiar to the Rhenish provinces, while in Belgium the cathedral of Tournai is one of the most striking monuments of this epoch.

Latterly in France the Romanesque has been successfully used in some large churches, among which are "St. Pierre de Montrouge" in Paris and "St. Jean" at Bar-le-Duc.

In America there was a brief period during which, in some cities, the Romanesque was applied to various buildings. Without doubt the happiest and most admired application of this style to the religious needs of modern America is found in Trinity Church, Boston, which shows traces of the influence of some of the late Romanesque churches of southern France and Spain.

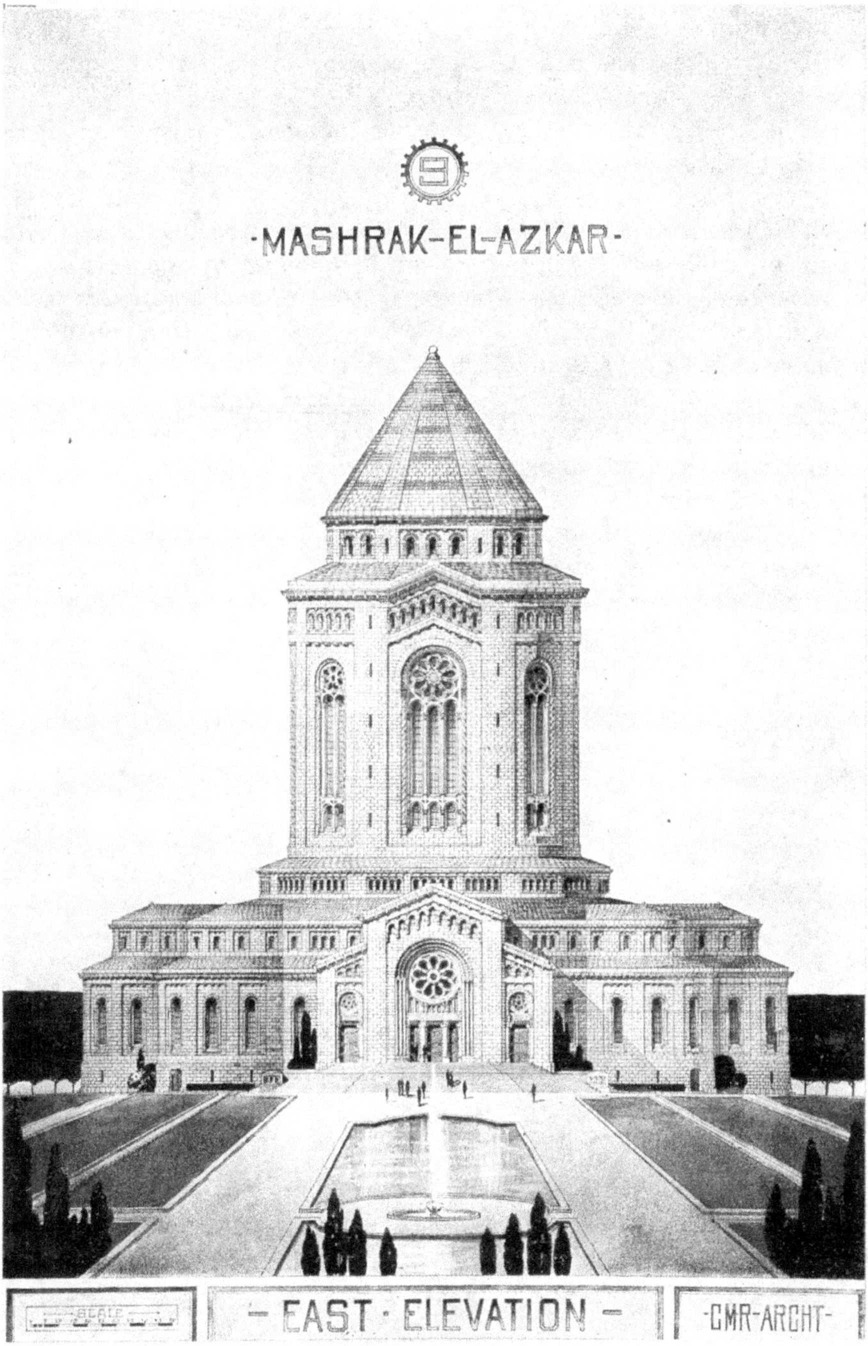

·MASHRAK–EL–AZKAR·

– SCALE –   – EAST · ELEVATION – || –CMR·ARCHT–

The architect has imagined this building in the Romanesque style to be constructed entirely of masonry.

The exterior is of light granite, including the conical roof of the cupola as well as the other roofs which are formed of slabs supported by the interior vaulting.

The interior is finished in a light colored stone with sculptured ornament, while a rich color effect will be obtained by stained glass.

The high central space is surrounded by an ambulatory divided by columns and piers (carrying the roof) into three aisles, from which open out large apses, each surrounded by a small ambulatory containing staircases connecting the main floor with the basement entrances. The upper stories of the central space or rotunda contain interior galleries, while about the base of the high central portion of the building runs a low exterior gallery enclosed by nineteen bays of five arcades each.

In making this design the architect has tried to retain the feeling of the Romanesque, which is somewhat more severe and less florid and exubriant than the Oriental styles and those of a later date of the Occident.

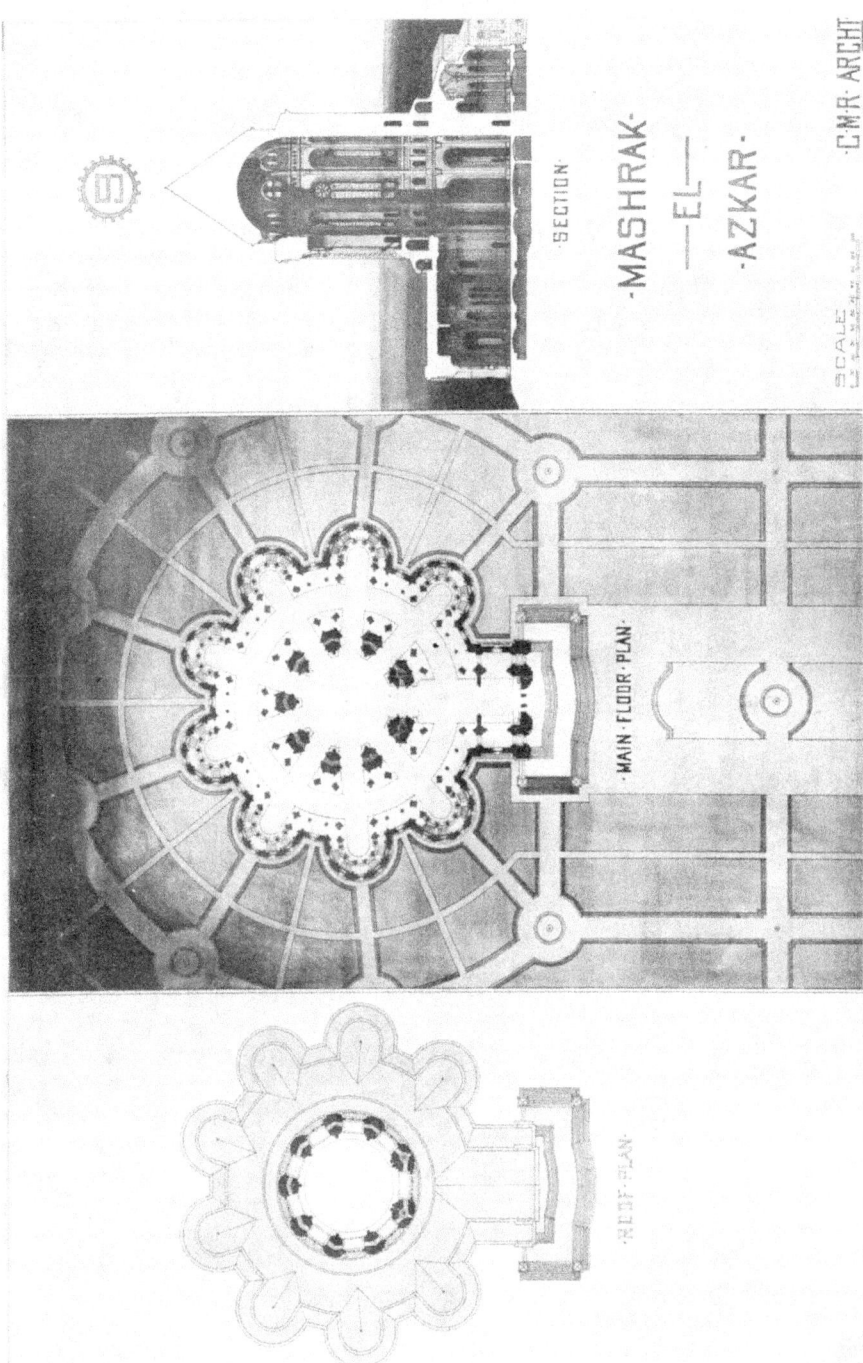

SECTION·

·MASHRAK·
——EL——
·AZKAR·

·C·M·R· ARCHT

SCALE

·MAIN·FLOOR·PLAN·

·ROOF·PLAN·

99

DESIGN NO. 7.

THE GOTHIC STYLE OF ARCHITECTURE.

THE GOTHIC STYLE OF ARCHITECTURE found its origin in the Romanesque period. Like other styles, its character has been greatly influenced by local conditions, temperamental, cultural, military, national, and, above all, religious. The forms peculiar to it are found in different stages of evolution in various parts of Great Britain and Europe, but nowhere did it attain the grandeur and structural development reached in northern France in the twelfth century. This was brought about by a people working under the influence of a common religious ideal, a mixed people in whom were combined and balanced the artistic and intellectual traits of southern, central, and western Europe under social and political conditions which made possible the building of such monuments as the cathedrals of Paris, Amiens, Rheims, and Chartres which, together with many other less generally known cathedrals and churches, testify to this period, brief in length, of the perfection of the Gothic style.

To the casual observer, the Gothic style is characterized by the pointed arch, windows filled with tracery, ribbed and groined vaulting, spires and turrets, flying buttresses, and mouldings and ornaments of a distinctive type; but to the student of this art the chiefest and most distinguishing characteristic which it embodies, and which no other style of architecture embodies, is its structural system of active mechanical parts so arranged that a perfect equilibrium is attained by the neutralization of opposing and balanced thrusts. Thus in the typical Gothic cathedral this principle of mechanical structure differentiates that style from previous styles wherein the stability of buildings depended upon the inert massiveness of walls to overcome any internal or external thrusts. In the Gothic wall surfaces have almost ceased to exist, the structure being one vast stone skeleton of piers, arches, and ribs which support the vaults of the roof. The tracery, taking the place of the walls, carries the protecting glass.

Gothic architecture in its complete structural development never existed outside of a comparatively small area in northern France, yet in many other parts of Europe the churches and cathedrals of that epoch attained grandeur, beauty, and charm not to be questioned, and the development of many motives and details peculiar to the period but secondary to the unique structural principle attained by the French.

In mentioning the Gothic, the cathedral of Cologne in Germany should not be overlooked. This building was directly prompted by the French examples at Amiens and Beauvais. It is not structurally related to any local architectural development, so cannot be considered to have been evolved upon German soil.

In the western ecclesiastical world there has been a reversion to certain characteristics of Gothic in many of the churches recently built. In America almost every city and town has several so-called "Gothic churches," but when one examines these structures he finds they are not really Gothic. They carry certain decorative features peculiar to the Gothic style, yet structurally they cannot be classed as Gothic because they do not conform to the principle of this style.

In France in recent decades Gothic has been revived according to the true construction of the original epoch in the Church of "Ste. Clotilde" at Paris. Completed some sixty years ago this church is perhaps the best known example of pure modern Gothic. It is structurally carried out in accord with the perfected Gothic principle. The Pilgrim church of "Bonsecours" at Rouen, and the churches of "St. Epvre" at Nancy, and "St. Vincent-de-Paul" at Marseilles, though smaller than "Ste. Clotilde," are good examples of the modern French revival of thirteenth century Gothic.

The architect has imagined this building in the Gothic style to be constructed entirely of masonry, with the exception of the roofs, which will be of a light metal construction resting upon the structural masonry. Both the exterior and interior will be of light standstone, sparingly but richly decorated with sculptured ornament, the color effect in the interior to be obtained by a richness of stained glass, the windows being so developed as practically to eliminate the wall space, which arrangement is characteristic of the Gothic.

The high central space contains two stories of triforium galleries, and upon the main floor is surrounded by an ambulatory divided by piers, which carry the overhead vaults into three aisles, out from which open polygonal apses forming, as it were, a series of chapels surrounding the building.

The exterior of the edifice is dominated by the central portion, which rises high above the roofs of ambulatory and chapels, the most striking feature of which is without doubt the flying buttresses, counteracting the thrust of the interior vaults, which, with the turrets and other structural as well as decorative elements of the design, give the building the character peculiar to the Gothic.

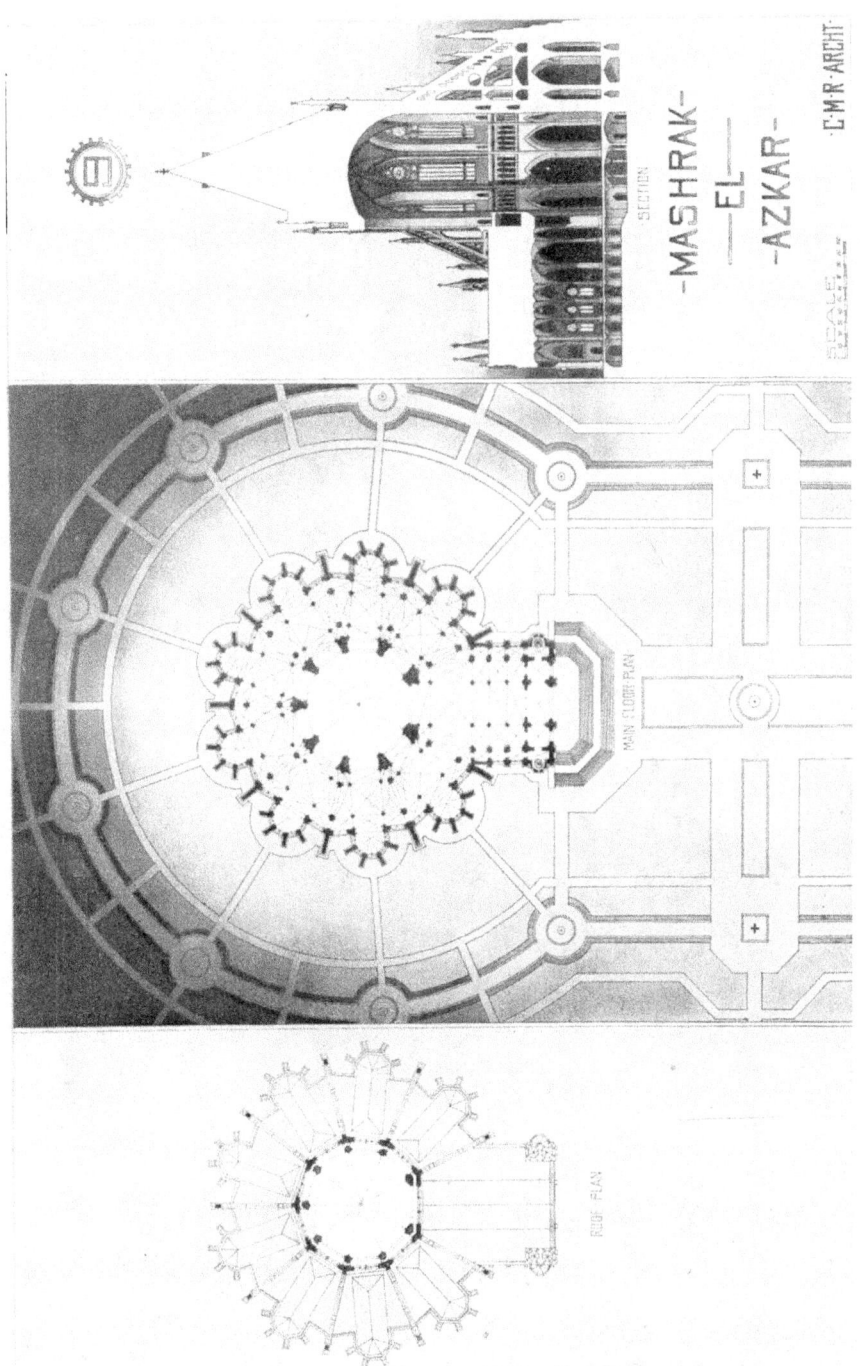

-MASHRAK-
—EL—
-AZKAR-

·C·M·R·ARCHT·

SECTION

MAIN FLOOR PLAN

ROOF PLAN

107

DESIGN NO. 8.
RENAISSANCE STYLE OF ARCHITECTURE.

THE RENAISSANCE STYLE OF ARCHITECTURE, or the application of classic forms to the needs of building, began with the revival of classic culture and traditions in Europe in the fourteenth, fifteenth, and sixteenth centuries, which had been latent and practically forgotten during the mediaeval ages.

With its general awakening first in Italy it spread to all parts of Europe, assuming many and various forms in different countries and under varying conditions, ranging from the simplicity of the almost pure classic through many variations to the flamboyant forms of Rococo and Louis XV, then to the more restrained Georgian and Colonial styles, and yet again to the florid extremes of the modern French Renaissance.

Some of the world-known ecclesiastical buildings of the Renaissance are "St. Peter's" church and "St. John Lateran," the cathedral of Rome, the "Escorial" in Spain, the "Tomb of Napoleon," the church of the "Sorbonne," and the more modern ones of "La Sainte Trinite" and "St. Vincent-de-Paul," and others in Paris, and St. Paul's Cathedral in London. In addition to these and other well known buildings practically every city where modern architecture has attained any development contains buildings, with Renaissance forms to some degree, so widespread in this day is the influence of this style.

The decorative possibilities of the Renaissance are without doubt more varied than those of any other style, this style having such a wide range of forms that there are practically no restrictions as to the materials which are in character with it.

-MASHRAK-EL-AZKAR-

+++ - EAST · ELEVATION - +++

The architect has imagined this building in the Renaissance style to be constructed of masonry, the exterior to be of light granite, the interior to be of stone and marbles, with sculptured ornament and mosaic treatments.

While the architectural details of this design are Renaissance, the general lines of the building approach the more eastern or oriental forms, which feeling the designer wishes to express in the interior treatment as well as upon the exterior of the building.

The high central rotunda, with its interior galleries, is surmounted upon the exterior by a dome with massive buttresses, about the base of which is a series of smaller domes which cover a corresponding number of smaller rotundas which encircle the central rotunda already described.

A series of large apses surround the building and are visible from the outside by their encircling porticoes and the half domes which cover them.

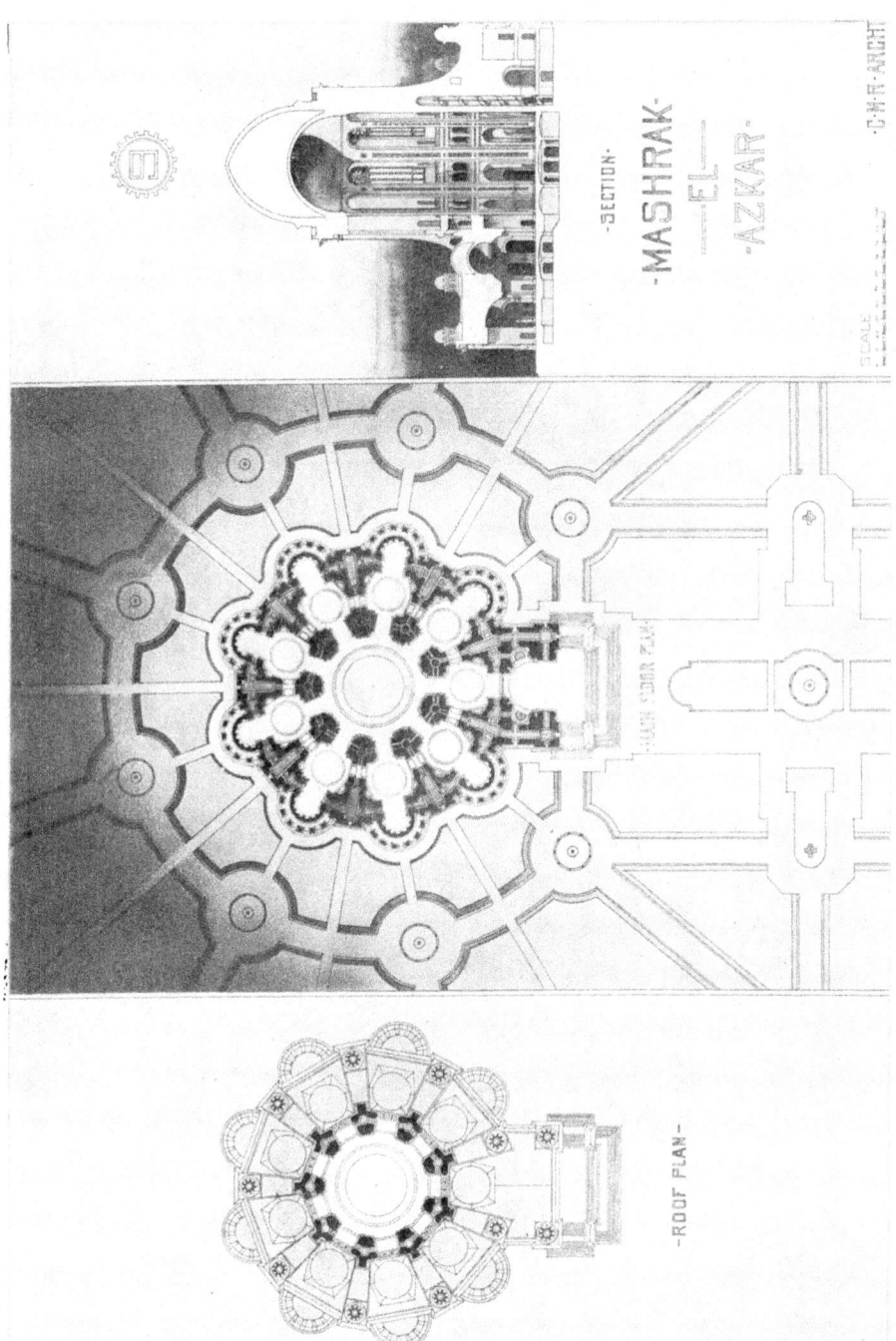

-SECTION-

-MASHRAK-
—EL—
-AZKAR-

-ROOF PLAN-

115

DESIGN NO. 9.

MODERN STYLE OF ARCHITECTURAL CONSTRUCTION.

THE MODERN STYLE OF ARCHITECTURAL CONSTRUC-
TION, product of the exigencies of building in America, but now being
emulated in other countries as well, as an art is yet in its earliest stages
of development. Structurally it is an application to present day needs
of the simple principles of timber construction known more or less to
builders in all ages, but which attained the highest architectural development and beauty in the so-called "half timbered" houses of the mediaeval
period.

In this period the art and the science of timber construction were so
happily combined as to have produced an architectural composition in
which the construction was apparent and the decoration so applied as
not to mask or to interfere with the mechanical structure, but to conform
to it, and to enhance its value by making it a thing of beauty. The
houses were built of timber, to which a light filling of masonry was
added to form the enclosing walls and partitions, and sometimes the
floors. When completed, these houses presented structures bony in
character, the parts of little resistance and the weight of the building
being carried by the timber framework. The difference between this
and the ordinary masonry and timber construction commonly built now-
a-days is that in these latter the enclosing walls of masonry are self-
supporting, and these not only carry their own weight, but also the
weight of the floors, roofs, and other parts of the building which rest
upon them.

In the business center of the typical American city it has been necessary to erect, for commercial purposes, buildings which are in many cases
great in height and small in lateral dimensions. This necessity, together
with considerations of economy of space and of building materials, has
produced the evolution of, first, the steel frame, and later the reinforced
concrete building now finding their development in the typical American
"sky piercer."

In the fireproof "sky piercer," and in the ordinary building constructed of timber, the structural principle is the same; namely, that there
are no self-supporting walls, but that the structural framework of the
building carries alike the walls, partitions, floors, and roof, and other
parts of the building. While the modern steel and concrete construction
is having its beginning in buildings of a type more utilitarian than beautiful, and up to this present time the best known examples of architecture
applied to this principle of construction are found in the factory and in
office buildings, rarely objects of beauty, yet there is every reason why
architects should seek to apply appropriate architectural treatments to

structures of this type, thus giving the modern steel and concrete structure architectural treatment which shall add to a building science already quite perfected the art of architecture which shall make these structures pleasing to the æsthetic sense of the passer-by in the measure that they are already practical and utilitarian.

In this style of architecture the possibilities of surface decoration, both exterior and interior, are almost without limit. Stucco, stone facing, brick, terra cotta, mosaic, etc., are all applicable and in harmony with the character of the structure.

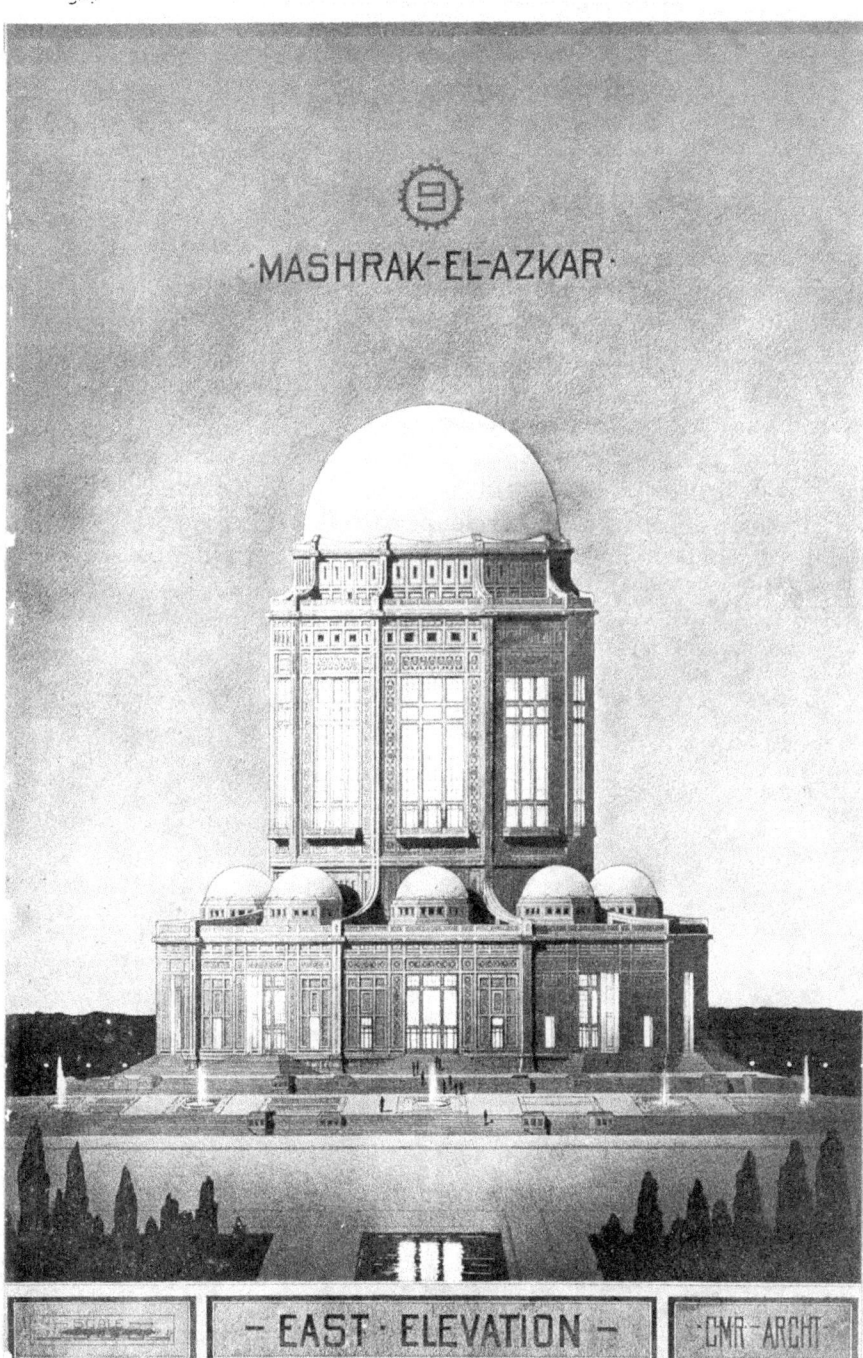

- EAST · ELEVATION -

The architect has imagined this building to be of reinforced concrete of the most improved and modern construction.

The exterior is to be encrusted with terra cotta and tiles, with stone casing near the ground. The interior to be likewise, treated with terra cotta and tiles, enriched by marble casings and mosaic decorations.

The high central rotunda with its galleries is surrounded by a series of smaller rotundas, and these in turn, upon the main floor, by a loggia which encircles the building, connecting the nine porticoes.

As in character with this style of construction, it will be seen that the wall supports in the plans are quite small in comparison with the floor areas, thus giving an air of lightness of structure attained in no other style, though approached in the Gothic.

In this design the architect has attempted to show frankly in the exterior and interior treatment of surfaces the character and lines of the internal structure of the skeleton and walls, thus trying to put into one homogeneous whole the architectural decoration and the mechanical structure.

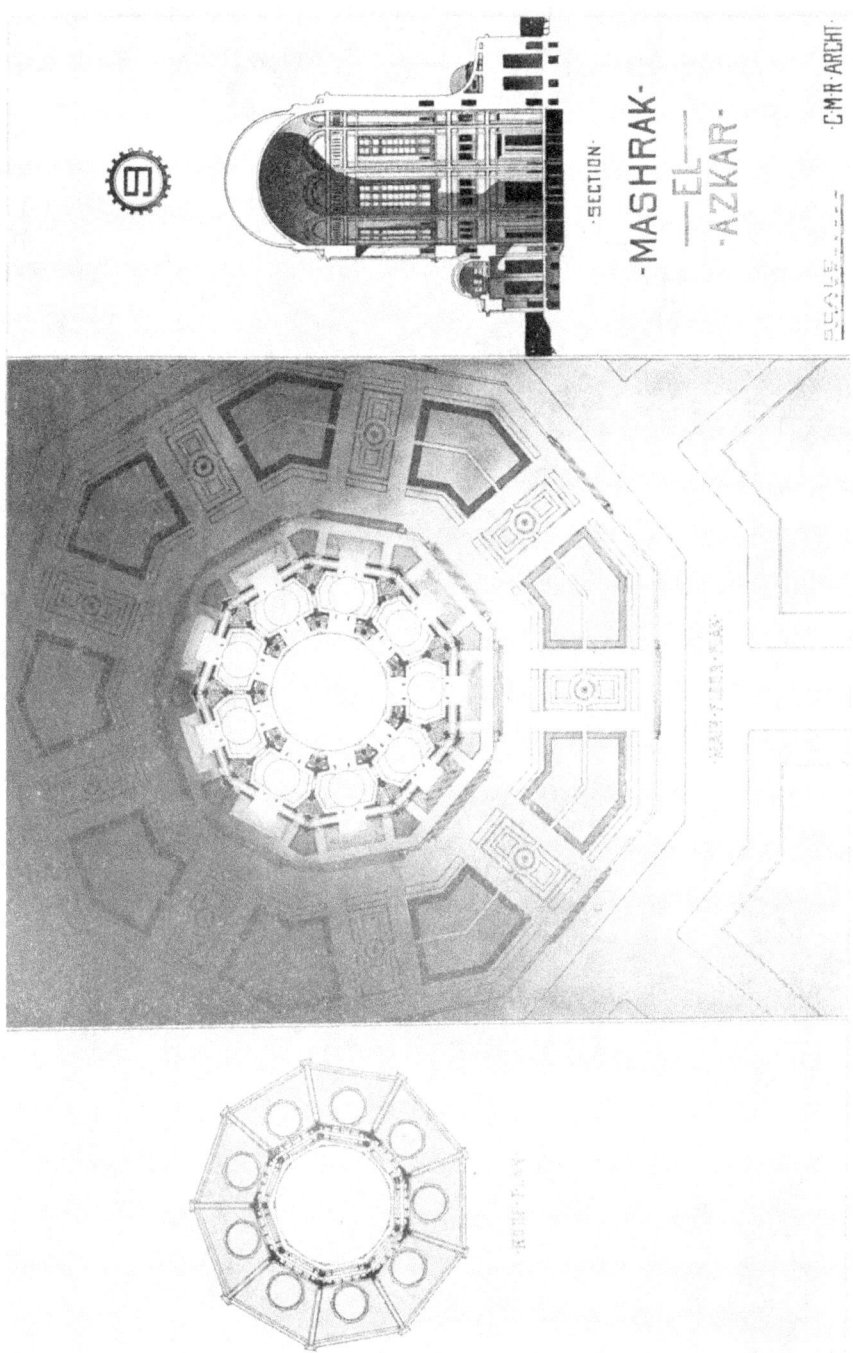

-SECTION-

-MASHRAK-
——EL——
-AZKAR-

C.M.R.ARCHT.

SCALE

123